# The Colour of Steam

Series Editor Nigel Trevena

**Volume Five**

# London Midland in The Fells

by DEREK HUNTRISS

Designed by Nigel Trevena
Typeset by Delta Graphics (0326) 76044
Printed by Century Litho, Penryn, Cornwall

ISBN 0 906899 18 4    First Published 1986

Published by
ATLANTIC TRANSPORT PUBLISHERS
Chough House River Street Truro
Cornwall TR1 2SJ England

## Introduction

August 11th 1968 is a date very much embedded in the minds of a whole generation of Britain's steam railway enthusiasts. Not only did it mark the end of regular use of steam locomotives on British Railways, it also marked the end of what had become a way of life to numerous steam railway enthusiasts.

Throughout the 1960s the demise of steam was accelerating and the day when it would cease altogether was getting closer. In a bid to record the last workings on film, many photographers made weekly pilgrimages to photograph yet another 'LAST', as classes became extinct and lines closed or became devoid of steam.

It was very fitting that steam's last stronghold was in the north west of England and that right to the very last day there was steam in the Fells, the final working being a '15 Guinea Special' from Liverpool to Carlisle which included a return journey over the Settle and Carlisle route.

During the latter years of steam, locomotives were generally filthy, run down and often devoid of name and numberplates. In order to secure a better then average photograph, several groups of enthusiasts formed volunteer cleaning parties and would spend many twilight hours polishing the pride back into many locomotives, returning them to pristine condition for their eleventh hour duties.

One particular group whose activities became legend from Aberdeen to Aberystwyth was the MNA or Master Neverers Association, the meaning of the title 'Neverer' not being abundantly clear, but suggesting that some enthusiasts 'Never' bothered. The most famous of the MNA's activities were the weekly Jubilee cleaning sessions at Leeds Holbeck when those prestigious locomotives were returned to their former duties hauling relief trains over the Settle and Carlisle route during the summer of 1967.

It is to one of this group that this book is dedicated, the late Paul Riley. A prolific photographer whose efforts to produce the ultimate 'master shot' are now almost legend, he was probably one of the most forward thinking photographers of his day, pioneering the use of long focus lenses to portray steam locomotives in their most dynamic form.
*Derek Huntriss*

FRONT COVER: LMS Coronation Pacific No.46245 *City of London* speeds across Dillicar troughs with the lightweight Workington portion of the 'Lakes Express', 13th July 1963. *Photo: Peter Fitton*

BACK COVER: On 12th August 1967, Stanier 5 No.45027 struggles the last few yards towards Ais Gill summit through weather conditions typical of the Settle and Carlisle line. *Photo: Derek Huntriss*

TITLE PAGE: 8F No.48448 blasts out of 265 yard Holme Tunnel on the 1 in 68 climb to Copy Pit summit, 24th February 1968. *Photo: Paul Riley*

ABOVE: Icy conditions at Shap Wells see Britannia Pacific No.70024 *Vulcan*, bereft of nameplates, being assisted with a northbound freight by Standard 4 No.75030, 20th December 1967. *Photo: Peter Fitton*

# Carlisle

RIGHT: 29th August 1962, and one of Carlisle Kingmoor shed's Princess Royal Pacifics stands in the centre road at the north end of Citadel station prior to making the ascent of both Beattock and Gleneagles banks with the 10.00 am Euston to Perth express. With only weeks to go before her withdrawal No.46203 *Princess Margaret Rose* retains her nameplates and is maintained in good external condition. The small bracket located on the cabside below the window is a remnant of a short-lived BR scheme in the 1950s and was intended to carry the name of the driver. *Photo: Peter Fitton*

BELOW: Carlisle, the gateway to Scotland, is a focal point for Anglo-Scottish traffic. With only three through platforms with their limited accommodation, there was always a headache for the operating department during the height of the summer with reliefs to many of the Anglo-Scottish expresses. Stanier Coronation Pacific No.46248 *City of Leeds* is waiting for an extra coach to be added to a relief to the southbound 'Midday Scot', well known to students of the LNWR as the 'Corridor'. A 10th August 1962 picture. *Photo: J. Neville Simms*

# Standard ending

BELOW: The high footplate of this 9F 2-10-0 clearly exposes the wheels and valve gear as it rests between duties at Carlisle Kingmoor motive power depot, where so many of the class ended their days, on 8th October 1966.

The 9F was probably the most successful BR standard type locomotive design and the last standard type to be constructed, but sadly it was destined to be very short lived. Many of the class had quite tragically short careers, being victims of the Modernisation Plan, and were still in excellent condition when withdrawn from service. In fact, during the course of 1965 the Western Region withdrew its entire allocation of the class which included some engines which had been built little more than five years earlier. By the end of 1966, half the class had gone. *Photo: Derek Huntriss*

OPPOSITE: After lengthy preparation by the MNA enthusiast group at Carlisle Kingmoor motive power depot, Britannia Pacific No.70013 *Oliver Cromwell* was turned out to work what became the last steam hauled passenger train over Shap, a football supporters' special leaving Carlisle at 9.45 am on 26th December 1967.

On the northern climb towards Shap the morning mists over Strickland Woods have risen as No.70013 blasts along on its 13 coach train to Blackpool South, from where No.70013 had to return to Kirkham tender first in order to proceed to Blackpool North for turning and servicing.

On the return leg of its journey north, the train stopped at Tebay to obtain banking assistance, but none being available, No.70013 made a spectacular unassisted ascent of Shap with its 451 ton train.

A decision to preserve No.70000 *Britannia* was dropped following vandalism whilst in store and No.70013 became the final Britannia Pacific on BR. It had been given a major overhaul at Crewe Works in January 1967 when it was fully repainted and since it was the last locomotive to be overhauled for BR at Crewe a small ceremony took place on 2nd February 1967 when it was returned to traffic. A period of railtour and special train workings followed, culminating with the engine working one leg of the final BR steam special over the section from Manchester to Carlisle. *Photo: Paul Riley*

# Kingmoor twilight

Monday 1st January 1968 was the date which heralded the opening of a new diesel depot simply known as Carlisle. In turn this meant the complete closure of Carlisle Kingmoor depot (12A) and brought to an end the regular use of steam traction over Shap and the Settle and Carlisle routes. Apart from the retention of No.70013 *Oliver Cromwell,* it also marked the end of the Britannia Pacifics.

Once again prepared for duty by the MNA, Britannia Pacific No.70045 *Lord Rowallan* is sporting paper nameplates as she climbs the northern approach to Shap with a Carlisle to Manchester parcels working in December 1967. The train is approaching Shap village with the Lake District fells in the background.

No.70045 was one of a batch of ten Britannias constructed at Crewe during 1954 and was fitted with one of the BR1D flush-sided tenders which had steam operated coal pushers, a capacity of 4,725 gallons of water and 9 tons of coal. Another improvement which was adopted on this batch was a revised cab/tender arrangement which was made to improve cab comfort and reduce the noise and draughts which had been a source of complaint from footplatemen who drove the initial batch of Britannias.

*Lord Rowallan's* final duty was to haul the 13.10 Carlisle-Skipton goods on 30th December 1967, the last steam hauled freight to leave Carlisle before Kingmoor depot was closed.
*Photo: Paul Riley*

## Fives at the summit

ABOVE: In 1967 the use of steam motive power over Shap was generally restricted to freight and parcels duties except during the summer timetable when there were extra Saturdays only passenger turns which included reliefs to many of the regular expresses. On 22nd July 1967, Stanier 5 No.45072 staggers over Shap Summit with 1M32, the Saturdays only southbound 1.26 pm Glasgow to Morecambe train. During the course of the 31.4 miles from Carlisle to Shap Summit at 916 feet above sea level, No.45072 gradually lost power, finally stopping for a blow up just before the summit.

RIGHT: In contrast, Stanier 5 No.44876 appears to have made light work of the southern climb to Shap Summit on the same day with 1L27, the 11.55 am Euston to Carlisle, which it had taken over at Crewe. Having breasted Shap Summit after the four mile climb of 1 in 75 from Tebay her fireman can now take a breather on the down grades to Carlisle. The summer of 1967 became the last in which regular steam hauled passenger trains could be seen over Shap. *Photos: Peter Fitton*

OPPOSITE, TOP: One of the most memorable things about steam over Shap was the way in which northbound trains proclaimed their coming (and their passing) for a considerable length of time. On an autumn day such as this with the mists still lying in the valley bottoms and the noise of cars travelling along the A6 being hidden behind the next hill, it was only the distant crowing of whistles at Tebay that broke the silence. On 4th November 1967, Stanier 5 No.45353 was about to be assisted by Standard 4 No.75030 up to the summit. Their muffled exhausts could be heard until they rounded the corner at Greenholme when their efforts became more pronounced until they passed this popular location at Shap Wells and remained audible until the banker became detached at the summit.
*Photo: Derek Huntriss*

OPPOSITE, BOTTOM: Some five years earlier, on 4th August 1962, at the same location, Stanier Princess Royal Pacific No.46208 *Princess Helena Victoria* ascends unassisted with the 9.25 am Crewe to Aberdeen. No.46208 was one of six serviceable Princess Royal Pacifics to be unexpectedly returned to traffic at the end of January 1962, reportedly to overcome a serious shortage of English Electric Type 4s on the west coast main line. They remained in traffic on mainly top class passenger work until the commencement of the winter timetable left only one Princess Royal in service, No.46200 *The Princess Royal,* which was finally condemned in November 1962. *Photo: Peter Fitton*

ABOVE: As trends in railway freight traffic have altered over the years one type of business that has totally disappeared is the carriage of livestock.

Stanier 5 No.45444 approaches Scout Green in October 1967 with a northbound freight which includes several examples of cattle trucks, a type of vehicle now just a memory on British Railways. *Photo: Paul Riley*

**Memories of Shap**

During the last month of steam working over Shap,
December 1967, the 8.20 am Ribble Sidings to
Carlisle was one of the last remaining steam turns.
With today's 25kv electric traction hauling trains past
this setting at Greenholme at speeds approaching 100
mph, in both directions, it is difficult to recollect that
scenes like this ever took place.

Recorded for ever in December 1967 on
Kodachrome II, 25 ASA film, Paul Riley's art is seen
at its brilliant best. He has exercised great skill in
holding steady his Prinz 400mm telephoto lens. This
long focus lens has heightened the drama of the
backlit exhausts of both train and banking engines,
superbly exposed for maximum effect.
*Photo: Paul Riley*

**The power ....**

## .... and the glory

9th December 1967 had been a day of vicious weather conditions typical of the northern fell region. Overnight, frost had given way to a howling blizzard which only subsided just before the last steam hauled working of the day pressed forward over Shap.

The work of the banking engine is clearly depicted here as the late afternoon sunlight catches Standard 4 No.75030 giving its best assistance to a northbound mineral train near Greenholme.

For many years banking duties on Shap had been entrusted to the capabilities of Fowler 2-6-4Ts, some fitted with side window cabs, two in tandem frequently assisting the heavier workings. Tebay motive power depot finally closed to steam traction from 1st January 1968 being replaced briefly by Clayton Type 1 diesels.

In the 1860s and 1870s a somewhat alarming method of banking was employed. As soon as the passing train had cleared Tebay the banking engine would pursue the train at speed, much to the amazement of the passengers. This practice usually made a very perceptible impact on the buffers of the moving train and was finally abandoned after severe damage was experienced at the rear of a train.
*Photo: Paul Riley*

# In the gorge

The epic scenery of the Lune Gorge gives a classic setting for this picture, dated 29th July 1967. The river, flowing swiftly between massive rocks, is sandwiched between mountains on either side. To the west are the Borrowdale Fells (not to be confused with those in Lakeland) with Jeffrey's Mount rising to over one thousand feet. To the east lie the Howgills, an amazingly unknown and little visited range of hills.

The summer of 1967 brought the annual increase in passenger traffic which meant that, once more, steam hauled passenger trains could be seen tackling the gradients on both sides of Shap Summit. Here, Stanier 5 No.45347 hauling the summer SO 9.25 am Blackpool to Glasgow takes water from Dillicar troughs immediately prior to the ascent to Shap Summit. It is seen passing D6826 which is hauling the summer SO 9.00 am Newcastle to Blackpool.

Sadly, although probably inevitably, the Lune Gorge was chosen as the route for the M6 motorway, which is now never more than one mile from the railway, all of the way between Grayrigg and Carlisle. Whereas the railway blended well with the landscape, the greater scale of the motorway has destroyed the dramatic effect. *Photo: Derek Huntriss*

13th July 1963: against the backdrop of the Howgill Fells, Royal Scot No.46118 *Royal Welch Fusilier* is threading the northern end of the Lune Gorge before taking water on Dillicar troughs, having made the most of the favourable gradients to build up the maximum amount of speed for the steep climb ahead. No.46118 is hauling 1X68, a special working from Kensington Olympia taking delegates to the Keswick Convention, an Evangelical event held annually during July since 1875. This special working could be seen on its return trip after the convention ended some two weeks later.

Steam locomotives passing over Dillicar troughs often gave the photographer the spectacle of water overflowing from a full tender and mixing with smoke and steam against the backcloth of mountains to create an almost mystical effect.

With the onset of the diesel age the level of water in the troughs was lowered in an attempt to reduce the corrosive effect on the tracks. The sight of water overflowing from locomotive tenders became less common except when an unnamed enterprising photographer decided to jam open the control valve to secure an all time master shot and also give an unexpected early bath to the occupants hanging out of the windows of the first three coaches of the 'Border Countryman' railtour. *Photo: Peter Fitton*

# Scot at Dillicar

## The Settle & Carlisle: beneath Cross Fell

LEFT: Two and a half miles north of Appleby is the beautiful Long Marton viaduct built to cross Trout Beck, a tributary of the River Eden. The structure's native red and white sandstone was quarried at nearby Dufton Wood.

Snow capped Cross Fell provides an attractive backcloth as one of Carlisle Kingmoor's Ivatt 4 2-6-0s returns north from Appleby with a permanent way train on 8th November 1967. This class of locomotive was Ivatt's final design. The last new type introduced by the LMS prior to nationalisation, it was a modern replacement for the numerous ageing 0-6-0 freight engines including Fowler's standard type. The new Class 4 broke away from LMS convention with the running plate being placed high up on the boiler flanks giving easy access to the wheels and motion.
*Photo: J. Neville Simms*

## Last of the Pacifics

RIGHT: 5th February 1967 was a memorable day for enthusiasts wanting to see Pacific hauled passenger trains traversing the Settle and Carlisle route. On the previous day, the bi-annual Rugby Union International between Scotland and Wales was held in Edinburgh, and to return supporters to their native homeland BR had laid on six special workings, four of which were Britannia hauled south of Carlisle. Routed via Carlisle, Hellifield and Blackburn, they rejoined the west coast main line south of Preston.

One of these specials, hauled by Britannia No.70010 *Owen Glendower*, is seen on the northern ascent to Ais Gill passing through Kirkby Stephen West, which like so many other stations on the Settle and Carlisle route was built some distance from the settlement it purported to serve.
*Photo: Peter Fitton*

## The Long Megs

RIGHT: Perhaps the finest sight in the last few months of regular BR steam over the Settle and Carlisle was the Long Meg Sidings to Widnes anhydrite traffic, usually powered by a 9F 2-10-0.

With five miles of unbroken climbing at 1 in 100 to go before reaching the summit at Ais Gill, the crew of 9F No.92249 can take little respite as they head their southbound Long Meg into Birkett Tunnel on 13th July 1967. The 424 yards long Birkett Tunnel is sited on the Great Pennine Fault and in its making, shale, iron, coal and a workable vein of lead were all discovered.

After leaving the tunnel, southbound trains emerge to take the traveller along Mallerstang, the railway offering the passenger much better views of Mallerstang Edge than those obtained by the motorist. *Photo: Derek Huntriss*

## Au revoir

RIGHT: Sunday 11th August 1968 marked the end of an era, with BR's last steam hauled train running over standard gauge track. 420 passengers paid fifteen guineas each for the 314 mile round trip from Liverpool to Carlisle, the price including a cold lunch, champagne and other refreshments, as well as a souvenir ticket and scroll.

The train was handled by four locomotives, the first being Stanier 5 No.45110 which stormed out of Liverpool Lime Street at the head of ten coaches, departing simultaneously with the 9.10 am electric hauled express to Euston. Two photographic stops were made en route to Manchester, the first being at Rainhill, the site of the 1829 locomotive trials, and the second at Parkside.

Britannia Pacific No.70013 *Oliver Cromwell* took over the train at Manchester Victoria for the journey to Carlisle via Blackburn, Hellifield and Ais Gill.

The return leg of this train was hauled by Stanier 5s Nos.44871 and 44781, seen here climbing along Mallerstang towards the crowds who had turned out at Ais Gill. *Photo: Derek Huntriss*

The Midland Railway took nearly six years, from 1869 to 1875, to complete its crossing of the Pennines from Settle to Carlisle and thereby opening its own route between England and Scotland. This spectacular line climbs to 1,169 feet above sea level at Ais Gill summit in the bare and windswept fells.

Against the impressive backdrop of Wild Boar Fell Stanier 8F No.48204 makes a fine sight on 4th November 1967 as it storms the last few yards to Ais Gill summit.

Ais Gill itself boasted nothing except a sort of cafe which never seemed to be open. The signalbox was one of many on the line that did not have running water laid on and at one time the local trains used to drop off water cans for the signalmen. Latterly, a spring near the signalbox was used. Night duty at this box was a very lonely business and the bobby would very often welcome tape recording enthusiasts who would try to record the passage of southbound trains struggling hard against the grade over the last five miles from Birkett Tunnel to the summit to the accompaniment of raucous bell codes.

Happily the saga of Ais Gill box has a pleasant ending. It has been relocated and restored at the Butterley base of the Midland Railway Project.
*Photo: J. Neville Simms*

## The loneliness of Ais Gill

On 4th November 1967, Stanier 8F No.48090 provided unusual motive power for the morning Long Meg Sidings to Widnes anhydrite working and had obviously encountered many mishaps on the northern ascent to Ais Gill as the time was well into the afternoon. No.48090 was observed taking 45 minutes for the six and a half mile climb from Kirkby Stephen to Ais Gill, stopping no less than three times for blow ups while climbing along Mallerstang. It is seen making better progress after crossing the road at Shaw Paddock before entering the 106 yard long Shotlock Hill tunnel against the mountain skyline of Wild Boar Fell.

The beerhead for visiting enthusiasts to the Ais Gill and Garsdale areas was (and still is) the Moorcock Inn near Garsdale. Having been rained off the fells on one occasion a visit to this hostelry coincided with local sheep dog trials and one could learn amongst other things the intricacies of sheep handling, knowledge of which would have been invaluable on many occasions when they decided to chew my guy ropes in the dead of night. *Photo: J. Neville Simms*

# 9F at Dent

RIGHT: A down freight on 14th July 1967, headed by 9F 2-10-0 No.92012, curves through Dent station and heads towards Ais Gill. This station is reached by a crazy, corkscrew road which climbs 450 feet in little more than half a mile. With a gradient of 1 in 5, it is commonly known as the Coal Road for it was originally built to serve coal pits, now long defunct, on Widdale Fell. The station, at 1,145 feet above sea level and the highest on any English main line, was built as close as possible to the village of Dent, over four miles away. *Photo: Derek Huntriss*

## Arten Gill viaduct

LEFT: Britannia Pacific No.70016 *Ariel* heads the northbound 9.20 am St Pancras to Glasgow across the lofty arches of Arten Gill viaduct, on 22nd July 1967. This was the only occasion during the summer of 1967 when this particular train was not handled by a Jubilee 5XP. Subsequently, the locomotive did not receive the usual servicing facilities provided by the MNA which were afforded to the Jubilees at Leeds Holbeck motive power depot.

No.70016 was one of several Western Region Britannias which had modified smoke deflectors in an attempt to improve the driver's vision. This followed the accident at Milton near Didcot in 1955 when as a result of an enquiry the handrails were attributed to impeding the driver's vision. They were removed and replaced with six holes cut into the plate and edged with brass. *Photo: Peter Fitton*

ABOVE: The LMS Jubilees, by virtue of their long association with the St Pancras to Glasgow 'Thames-Clyde Express' and St Pancras to Edinburgh 'Waverley', are synonymous with the Settle and Carlisle. In 1967 they had their swan song, working summer Saturday relief trains between Leeds and Carlisle, and with almost religious fervour a small group of the MNA spent their Friday nights polishing some pride back into the remaining members of this once numerous class.

No.45593 *Kolhapur* leaves a trail of exhaust as it coasts across Arten Gill viaduct with the 9.20 am St Pancras to Glasgow which it had taken over at Whitehall Junction, Leeds. A 19th August 1967 picture. *Photo: Derek Huntriss*

## Dent Head

High in the Pennines, Stanier 5 No.44727 makes light work of a southbound freight as it curves over Dent Head viaduct on the northern approach to Blea Moor tunnel. As seen here, from above the road which leads into the dale from Newby Head, its ten spans of graceful masonry, with a total length of 197 feet, blend well with the dale's setting of outbarns, dry stone walls and sheep. Standing at a height of 1,150 feet above sea level it is built from a lovely blue variety of locally quarried limestone.

In this 22nd July 1967 view, the closed Dent Head signalbox can be seen above the rear of the train. It was closed early in 1965 when all arms were removed from the signal posts in this section. An unusual piece of signalling was the gong on the down line in Blea Moor tunnel. It used to sound when the distant signal immediately beyond the northern portal was at danger. Drivers of express trains emerging from the tunnel like bats out of hell often had difficulty spotting this signal so the gong performed a vital function. *Photo: Peter Fitton*

# Wild Blea Moor

RIGHT: Southbound Long Meg hauled by Standard 9F 2-10-0 No.92058 approaches the northern portal of Blea Moor tunnel on 16th October 1967. The post which supported the Dent Head down distant is clearly seen in this photograph. Southbound crews always had difficulty in sighting the Blea Moor distant, hence the installation of the repeater signal which is visible at the north end of the tunnel. Today's visitor to this location would see a considerable transformation, the wild moorland scenery having been heavily forested. *Photo: J. Neville Simms*

BELOW: When exposed Blea Moor is not swept by driving rain, or lost in rolling mist, it can present an awe inspiring scene. Here, Stanier 8F No.48666 is making for the respite of Blea Moor after the gruelling 14 mile climb of 1 in 100 from Settle Junction, while 9F 2-10-0 No.92161 has brought a southbound Long Meg Sidings to Widnes anhydrite train up to the starter, 21st September 1966.

The line itself runs through squelching bogs on the flanks of Whernside which reaches the lofty altitude of 2,419 feet. *Photo: Peter Fitton*

# Blea Moor to Settle

OPPOSITE, TOP: 21st September 1966: with the eastern slopes of the 2,373 feet high flat topped summit of Ingleborough clearly visible, 9F 2-10-0 No.92017 makes its approach to lonely Blea Moor. Drivers of engines wishing to take water at Blea Moor would usually whistle, one long and three short when passing Horton or Dent. This was not, of course, with the intention of being heard at Blea Moor; the message was telephoned ahead so that if demands of traffic required it, the train could be put into the loop. *Photo: Peter Fitton*

OPPOSITE, BOTTOM: Jubilee No.45593 *Kolhapur* makes a stirring sight as it hauls the summer SO 9.20 am St Pancras to Glasgow over Ribblehead viaduct on 5th August 1967.

Taking five years to construct, the 440 yard, 24 arch viaduct had every sixth arch strengthened and built to larger dimensions using the logic that if one arch should ever fall only five would follow.

Today, the future of the Settle and Carlisle hangs in the balance, one of the main reasons for conjecture being the state of Ribblehead viaduct. The line over the viaduct has now been singled and trains restricted to 30 miles per hour. *Photo: Mike Collins*

BELOW: Maundy Thursday, 23rd March 1967, saw Jubilee No.45647 *Sturdee* at the head of the relief 'Thames-Clyde' express which it worked from Leeds to Glasgow St Enoch, possibly the last time a 5XP worked into Scotland in regular traffic. It is seen making a spirited departure from Settle in superb lighting conditions.

Once again the immaculate condition of this locomotive had been the responsibility of members of the MNA who, having worked all through the previous night at Leeds Holbeck, returned it to pristine condition with the adornment of a wooden nameplate. *Photo: Peter Fitton*

# Locos old and new

RIGHT: The 4-4-0 type of locomotive was a familiar sight on the Settle and Carlisle for over 70 years up to 1960. No.40685, seen here in a forlorn state at the back of Hellifield motive power depot on 24th April 1962, was one of the later developments of the class introduced by Sir Henry Fowler in 1928. This type of engine was used for piloting trains from Hellifield to Carlisle, and in their final years they were often seen hauling Hellifield to Blackburn local services. *Photo: Peter Fitton*

BELOW: Skipton station, seen from the west on 14th July 1967, sees Standard 4 No.75042 marshalling a train which had arrived from the Grassington branch. In the distance is the ridge which forms the western edge of Ilkley Moor. Formerly a Skipton 4F 0-6-0 working, the trip to Spencer's Lime Works Siding at Rylstone became one of the last steam-hauled branch workings in Britain. This former Midland Railway branch once had its terminus at Grassington and Threshfield and its passenger service ceased as long ago as 1930. *Photo: Derek Huntriss*

This rear three-quarter view shows excellent mechanical detail of Fowler 5X Patriot No.45505 *The Royal Army Ordnance Corps* leaving Wennington on the now lifted line to Lancaster on 24th April 1962. It was working the 10.47 am Leeds to Morecambe and Carnforth train, the Carnforth portion being worked forward by Stanier 3 2-6-2T No.40138. This view also shows footplate activity, the fireman hosing down the coal in the 7 ton, high straight-sided ex-Jubilee tender. Only two tenders of this type were fitted to Patriots: the first to No.45550 from May 1946 to April 1956, then to No.45539 from April 1956 to January 1958 when it was re-fitted to a Jubilee. The second tender was fitted to No.45551 between July 1958 and April 1960 and finally to No.45505 until its withdrawal in June 1962.

This engine was not named until 1947 but, had a 1943 scheme been implemented, the name *Wemyss Bay* would have been used. *Photo: Peter Fitton*

# Portrait of a Patriot

# Last rites at Windermere

LEFT: 1st August 1968 was the penultimate day of steam traction to Windermere and a little extra effort was needed to ensure Stanier 5 No.44894 looked its best. Overnight cleaning had taken place at Carnforth, but the final touches were added at Windermere station immediately prior to departure, the bewildered footplate crew looking on in amazement. Having boarded their refurbished steed they kindly agreed to provide an appropriate amount of black smoke at a pre-arranged location to add the final touch to this picture of their train leaving Windermere with parcels for Carnforth. *Photo: Derek Huntriss*

ABOVE: On 3rd August 1968, the final steam movement on the Oxenholme to Windermere branch returned from Kendal with only its brake van. Unusually for the last week of steam on BR, Stanier 5 No.44709 had arrived at Kendal in a very begrimed condition. With only a short turn round time at Kendal and only two of us available it was decided that we should clean one side only, the side that we would eventually photograph. Cleaning materials were quickly purloined and large quantities of oil were applied to give something resembling a clean locomotive. All this frantic activity was watched by several enthusiasts, whose accents identified their homes as being somewhere south of Watford. They were generally bemused by this now time honoured ritual and, even

after some verbal badinage and the throwing of oily rags, they could not be persuaded to take part. However, unfortunately for us, when we came to take our hard won picture, the train appeared sporting a Southern Region headcode indicating that the locomotive would have been better employed somewhere between Nine Elms and Clapham Junction. *Photo: Derek Huntriss*

# On Furness metals

ABOVE: There is little doubt that, in England, the most devious railway route of any importance is the former Furness Railway between Carnforth and Millom. Leaving the west coast main line at Carnforth, the Furness Railway branches north-north-west to Arnside, then turns west to cross the Kent estuary and continues south-west from Grange-over-Sands to Kents Bank. Skirting the northern edge of Morecambe Bay on 2nd August 1968, Standard 4 No.75048 heads for Ulverston with the morning pick-up freight shortly after leaving Carnforth. *Photo: Derek Huntriss*

RIGHT: Beginning its final year of active service on BR, Britannia Pacific No.70014 *Iron Duke* is seen on 3rd January 1967 in ex-works condition leaving Carnforth motive power depot. It has always remained a mystery why the turntable should have been left set at such a peculiar angle. As is well known, this depot has survived in the form of Steamtown and is now the home of many preserved engines. When it closed in August 1968 it was one of the final three depots which had an allocation of steam, the other two being Lostock Hall and Rose Grove. *Photo: Peter Fitton*

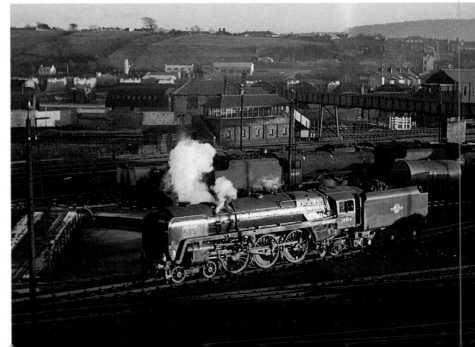

# ".... all the bloody way to Healey Mills."

With the closure of Workington, Carlisle and Tebay motive power depots from 1st January 1968, steam in the fells moved further south and Copy Pit on the Burnley to Todmorden route became one of the more popular locations where steam could still be seen fully extended.

The early hours of 24th February 1968 had seen fervent activity at Rose Grove motive power depot. The provisional wing of the MNA had once again been hard at work. There were four locomotives in steam on shed and not knowing which would work over Copy Pit, the decision was taken to clean all four. The pot of red paint finally ran out only two inches from the bottom of the buffer beam of Stanier 8F No.48448. These activities were carried out unbeknown to the footplate staff and, on signing-on, the driver of No.48448 was ecstatic about his 'ex-works' 8F. When questioned about providing black smoke at a particular location, he replied that "It'll clag all the bloody way to Healey Mills."

The locomotive and its train of empties are seen blasting along near Cliviger, the driver giving a star turn performance. It was always sad at this point in time that one day's star turns were very often in the following day's scrap lines. *Photo: Paul Riley*

## Todmorden to Burnley

The most impressive section of the Todmorden to Burnley line is where it crosses the county boundary from the West Riding of Yorkshire into Lancashire. The original single track branch was authorised by the Manchester and Leeds Railway in 1845, the first train running to Burnley Thorneybank on 12th November 1849. The following year saw a short extension opened to Gannow Junction near Rose Grove where the Todmorden line joined the East Lancashire Railway's Colne to Preston route.

Here we see an unidentified Stanier 8F crossing the county boundary in February 1968, emerging from the 290 yard Kitson Wood tunnel directly on to the 13 arch Nott Wood viaduct. This train had originated at Healey Mills yard and is destined for Wyre Dock. Shortly after it left the Calder Valley line at Hall Royd Junction the train stopped at Stansfield Hall Junction in order to attach another Stanier 8F to the rear for banking assistance for the climb to Copy Pit summit. The ten mile link between Hall Royd and Gannow junctions is steeply graded and heavily engineered. From Stansfield Hall the line climbs at 1 in 65 for over two and a quarter miles before easing at Portsmouth to 1 in 100 until the summit at Copy Pit is reached four and a quarter miles from Hall Royd junction.

Intermediate stations on the Copy Pit line were all closed by 1961, the last to go being Burnley Manchester Road which had replaced the original Burnley Thorneybank in 1866. A local service operated between Todmorden and Rose Grove until 1965 after which the Todmorden to Stansfield Hall curve fell into disuse. *Photo: Paul Riley*

# Derby to Manchester

Steam working south-east of Manchester to Buxton finally came to an end with the closure of Northwich (8E), Trafford Park (9E) and Buxton (9L) motive power depots from 4th March 1968, when the surviving steam-hauled freight workings were handed over to diesel traction.

The Midland Railway's line between Derby and Manchester through the Peak District was by far the most spectacular journey that could be made in North Derbyshire, but sadly in 1967 the tracks were lifted over much of the route and only the magnificent civil engineering works remained as a reminder of its former presence. The Derby to Chesterfield route remains as an important Inter City route, but never matched its offspring for grandeur.

At the end of January 1968 single line working had been introduced between Chinley South Junction and Peak Forest as a result of engineering work in Dove Holes tunnel. On 27th January 1968, 8F No.48775 works forward past Chinley South signal box prior to reversing and crossing over to the down line. Dove Holes tunnel is 1,224 yards long and the seventh longest in the Peak District, the line climbing on a gradient of 1 in 90 through the tunnel which makes the southern portal an incredible 99 feet higher than the northern entrance.

For many years Midland and LMS 0-6-0s were the mainstay of most Midland freight services, but by 1968 the remaining coal, limestone and general traffic was handled by Stanier 8F 2-8-0s.

8F No.48775 was constructed at Crewe in 1937 as LMS No.8025 and was one of several 8Fs to see service overseas when it was requisitioned by the War Department in 1944. During its duties abroad it saw activity in Persia as No.41.184. When it finally returned to England it was not taken back into British Railways stock until 1957 when it was given the number 48775. *Photo: Derek Huntriss*

# 8F action

RIGHT: Above the southern approach to Dove Holes tunnel at Peak Forest lies a vast limeworks complex. After working double-headed with sister 8F No.48191 from Gowhole Yard on 21st October 1967, 8F No.48465 marshalls her lengthy coal train before working forward to Buxton. Once again both locomotives were cleaned by the MNA during the previous night at Buxton motive power depot.

Buxton 8F's duties were mainly confined to serving the needs of several quarries and limeworks located in the surrounding countryside. Whichever route they worked, hard climbing was the order of the day, from the cavernous excavations of Great Rocks Dale to the slippery 1 in 90 climb through Dove Holes tunnel. This was no territory for faint hearted locomotives.
*Photo: Derek Huntriss*

LEFT: On the former Midland Railway route from Manchester to Derby, Stanier 8F No.48327 approaches Chinley with a freight from the Manchester area, on 3rd February 1968. The previous night had seen frantic activity at Buxton motive power depot as members of the MNA returned sister engine No.48442 to immaculate condition. Attempts to photograph No.48442's outward trip from Buxton to Gowhole Yard had been thwarted by early morning fog and the uncleaned No.48327 headed the first train to appear in good light.

This section of the former Midland Railway route near Chinley was widened to accommodate four tracks in 1902 and the tunnel which had previously existed at Buxworth was demolished and replaced by a deep cutting. Present day improvements in motive power and reductions in traffic have once again seen a return to a straightforward double track layout, the two lines farthest from the camera having been removed.
*Photo: Derek Huntriss*

3rd February 1968, and once again Paul Riley's innovative skill has shown its reward. Cleverly framed in this snow covered signal the immaculate Stanier 8F No.48442 finally heads back towards Chinley in excellent lighting conditions, the previous night's efforts not going unrewarded.

Being one of the most successful 2-8-0 designs, the LMS 8Fs were used as a standard, being built for other companies during the Second World War until the evolution of the Riddles Austerity 2-8-0.

The Stanier 2-8-0s were rarely in the limelight and were almost always confined to freight and parcels duties, their main object in life being hard slog with heavy loads at relatively low speeds.

*Photo: Paul Riley*

## Cromford & High Peak

April 1967 marked the closure of most of the Cromford and High Peak line. During the month a number of society specials, consisting mainly of brake vans and open wagons, had been hauled by a pair of J94 0-6-0Ts over parts of the route.

30th April saw scores of photographers lining the 1 in 14 Hopton Incline as J94s Nos.68012 and 68006 made their first attempt to haul six brake vans up the grade. This attempt proved to be too much and the pair reversed to split the train before trying again. The final empty stock working is seen making an all out effort to successfully master the grade.

The Cromford and High Peak Railway had been opened throughout from Cromford to Whaley Bridge in 1831 linking the terminii of the Peak Forest Canal and the Cromford Canal and crossing typically bleak Derbyshire moorland between these two waterways. At the time of opening there were five inclines on the ascent from Cromford to the summit near Ladmanlow and four whilst descending to Whaley Bridge.

Early traffic carried was mainly local limestone from the many quarries in the area although the line had been used for carrying coal, bricks, bone-manure and water.

For a period in the mid-19th century passengers had been permitted to use the line travelling in what was called a 'fly', a brake van with seats. This practice was discontinued after a fatal accident involving a passenger in 1877.

*Photo: Derek Huntriss*

Ex WD 2-8-0 Austerity No.90503 in full cry in an autumn landscape, the plume of its exhaust compensating for its lacklustre paintwork as it heads a mixed freight towards Chesterfield, shortly after leaving Ambergate on 3rd December 1966. This Riddles Ministry of Supply 'Austerity' 2-8-0 design was based on the Stanier 8F 2-8-0, but largely because of the need to make economies in materials and ease manufacturing methods, the final appearance was drastically different. *Photo: Derek Huntriss*

# Finale

Steam working over Copy Pit had finished just after midday on 17th February 1968. Burnley had beaten Manchester United 2-1 at Turf Moor and, before a long journey back to the Midlands, a final look was taken at Rose Grove motive power depot as several 8Fs simmered in the yard against a sunset over Huncoat power station.

Closing on 4th August 1968, Rose Grove was one of the final three BR depots to retain an allocation of steam locomotives. Normally a busy depot with duties that included a frequent service of coal trains between Burnley and Burn Naze, it also served through traffic between Preston and Healey Mills over Copy Pit. In addition, there were the heavy trip workings to Padiham power station and the supply of banking engines to Todmorden. These and some express freight workings to the Manchester area kept about 25 8Fs and a handful of Stanier Black 5s fairly busy. Amongst its allocation at the demise of steam was Stanier 8F No.48773, a locomotive with an incredibly chequered history, now preserved on the Severn Valley Railway as LMS No.8233. No.48773 was the last locomotive to be in steam at Rose Grove, its final duty on BR being to work the LCGB 'Farewell' special from Blackburn to Carnforth on 4th August 1968.
*Photo: Derek Huntriss*

## ACKNOWLEDGMENTS

The compilation of this book has been greatly aided by the generous contributions of the photographers credited in these pages. Special thanks to Peter Fitton, who provided a wealth of fine material, and to Nigel Trevena for his professional guidance and encouragement.     *Derek Huntriss*